CW01496791

THE BASICS OF MINISTRY SERIES

GUIDE FOR SACRISTANS

Christina Neff

LITURGY
TRAINING
PUBLICATIONS

ACKNOWLEDGMENTS

GUIDE FOR SACRISTANS © 2001 Archdiocese of Chicago: Liturgy Training Publications, 1800 North Hermitage Avenue, Chicago, Illinois, 60622-1101; 1-800-933-1800; orders@ltp.org; fax 1-800-933-7094. All rights reserved.

Visit our website at www.ltp.org

David A. Lysik was the editor of this book. Audrey Novak Riley was the production editor. Anna Manhart designed the *Basics of Ministry* series, and Kari Nicholls typeset this volume in Goudy. It was printed by Printing Arts Chicago in Cicero, Illinois. Cover photo and photos on pages 21 and 28 by Christina Neff; photos on pages 1, 7, 10, 37, 41 and 46 by Bill Wittman; photo on page i by Antonio Pérez.

05 04 03 02 01   5 4 3 2 1

ISBN 1-56854-279-8

EGSAC

Contents

THE MINISTRY OF THE SACRISTAN

This is a book about a ministry that has only recently begun to come into its own and to be appreciated for its tremendous potential—the ministry of the sacristan. The role of the contemporary sacristan in the life of the parish is an active one, and involves a good amount of creativity, organizational skill and diplomacy. This dynamic position is a relatively new development; the sacristy has likely long been considered little more than a dressing room or storage area, and the sacristan seldom more than its caretaker. But much has changed in recent years, and the sacristan is emerging as a valued minister and parish staff member who not only provides but coordinates the hands-on work a parish needs in order to celebrate its liturgy.

This book is intended as a guide for those already serving as sacristans, as well as for those contemplating entering this ministry. It is also meant to help parish leaders imagine and envision a new, broader paradigm for the ministry of sacristan. In some small way, too, it is hoped that this book will affirm and nourish the spirits and imaginations of sacristans. For we owe them a great deal: They keep our Easter fires burning, and they prepare the books; they fill our fonts with living waters, and they tend and make ready fragrant oils, heady incense and beautiful clothes. They set out the bread and pour the wine. In short, they make a room that invites the world to come to the table.

The role of the sacristan

Our appreciation and understanding of the role of the sacristan has developed hand-in-hand with our growing understanding of the teaching of the Second Vatican Council (1962–1965) that all the members of the church "should be led to take that full, conscious, and active part in liturgical celebrations which is demanded by the very nature of the liturgy" (*Constitution on the Sacred Liturgy*, 14). Since "in the restoration and development of the sacred liturgy the full and active participation by all the people is the paramount concern" (CSL, 14), the worshiping community needs ministers to help it realize this goal. One such minister is the sacristan.

Think for a moment of the bold woven textiles of the native peoples of the Southwestern United States. When we see these cloths and admire their beauty, we are often not immediately aware of the hours of labor that went into each piece. We also might not be aware of the many component actions and parts that contributed to the whole. We see the finished product and do not think too much about all the decisions the weaver had to make and all the work that had to be done: the gathering and dyeing of the yarns; the inspiration and laying out of the design the manipulation of yarn and loom, the diligent, focused eye. But for the cloth to come into existence, diverse materials and actions needed to be coordinated and interrelated.

The ministry of the sacristan is a bit like the work of the weaver. In order for all the members of a community of faith to take their full, conscious and active part in liturgical celebrations, there needs to be someone who prepares and oversees the things of the liturgy. There needs to be someone who gathers up the diverse things of the liturgy, readies them and renders them useful to the community gathered in the living prayer of the liturgy. This someone is the sacristan.

In a community of faith where the full and active participation of all in the liturgy is the paramount concern, the sacristan is necessarily much more than a behind-the-scenes caretaker of napkins and candle wax. The sacristan is to know the meaning and purpose of the liturgy as well as the needs of the particular liturgical assembly, and to work carefully to see the liturgy's ends realized by providing the members of the assembly with the tools they need. The sacristan keeps a vigilant eye on the entire house for the church and a ready hand on the whole of the liturgy's environment. Through sustained presence and action, the sacristan helps the community to realize a continuity in its practice of common prayer.

Qualities of a sacristan

A sacristan whose ministry extends beyond the confines of the sacristy—as it must—will be faced with a variety of situations and circumstances that call for a wide array of skills. Not only does the sacristan need to be handy and adept at preparing the physical things of the liturgy, he or she needs to be comfortable communicating and working with people. At all times, strong organizational skills are indispensable. In addition, the nature of the ministry requires other qualities of the sacristan.

Team member

As a sacristan, you are related to a group of fellow parishioners who work in some leadership capacity with regard to the parish's liturgy. This group may take several forms, depending on local needs and resources. In many parishes there is a liturgy board, or commission, that meets regularly to assess the parish's liturgies, make recommendations and provide direction. The chairpersons of the various "working committees" (lectors, ushers, art and environment, ministers of communion, musicians, catechists, preachers, and so forth) would likely be members of this liturgy commission, along with the parish clergy and other members at large. In other parishes, the work of various committees or ministries may be organized under the direction of a liturgy coordinator, or a team of people responsible for various areas of parish life.

Whatever the local organization model, the important point is that you as the sacristan do not work in isolation; you are one among others in your parish with leadership positions related to the liturgy. In order to perform your ministry effectively, it is vital that you be a member of the group that has parish liturgy leadership responsibilities. It is essential that you think of yourself as a member of this team, and that your presence on the team is expected. As the sacristan, you will need the "big picture" of the parish's liturgy that membership on the liturgy leadership team will provide. Without this active membership on the parish liturgy commission, your ministry simply will not be as effective as it could be.

An ordered outlook

Being a sacristan necessarily entails keeping the house in order. Your desire and ability to ensure that the things of the liturgy are clean, organized, inventoried and easily accessible is fundamental. There is little (if anything) that is hypothetical about your ministry; yours is a practical, hands-on service that demands solid organizational skills. Not only should you know what the parish uses in its liturgy and where these items are kept, but you should organize the parish's resources so that they are accessible to others who may need them in your absence.

Flexible schedule

One very important requirement of your ministry is your availability to work on Saturday afternoons and evenings, all day Sunday, during the paschal Triduum, and on such days as Ash Wednesday, Thanksgiving, All Saints, All Souls, Christmas and New Year's Day. Basically, you work the very hours that most people do not. In some parishes, especially larger ones with several Sunday liturgies, having two parish sacristans is a good way to distribute the Saturday–Sunday workload as well as a way to cover needs in the event of planned or unplanned absences. One good beginning strategy is for the parish liturgy coordinator to make a comprehensive list of all the liturgies requiring a sacristan, and to work from that list when deciding the number of sacristans the parish needs.

Spirituality and the sacristan

Many of those drawn to the ministry of sacristan describe themselves as action-oriented people who want to "do what they can" for the parish and to become closer to Christ in the liturgy of the church. Sacristans willingly take on a myriad of tasks, and are unafraid to commit themselves to the body of Christ through a repeated presence and participation at the liturgy—most often at back-to-back liturgies. The texts of the prayers, scripture readings and songs used during the liturgy become imprinted on the sacristan. Over the course of the sacristan's ministry, the images, metaphors, symbols and rhythms of the liturgy fuse with the sacristan's faith experiences in a concentrated way and form a rich source for spiritual reflection.

In addition, the sacristan is in a continual relationship with other parish ministers, as well as with the members of the entire assembly. In this way the sacristan is given many opportunities to practice the lessons of the liturgy, to love and serve Christ in the members of his body time and time again, Sunday after Sunday.

The ministry of the sacristan is a multi-faceted one. It is a work of integration and coordination, of giving attention to all God's holy people gathered for liturgy and to the things they need for their prayer. In some sense, the sacristan is a sort of linchpin for liturgy, gathering and holding together diverse elements for the benefit of the assembly's liturgical celebration. This is fertile ground for the spiritual nourishment of those who take on this ministry.

RESPONSIBILITIES AND WORKING RELATIONSHIPS

The sacristan must be ready to execute a number of varied tasks, as well as to interact effectively with all who gather for the liturgy. From the moment the sacristan opens the doors of the church until the time the last light is turned off, the sacristan's work can be depended on to be constant and sometimes fast-paced. The prime responsibilities of the sacristan are attending to the needs of the gathered assembly, maintaining all in good order for the liturgy at hand, facilitating the entrance procession, keeping watch, cleaning up and closing the church at the conclusion of the day's liturgies.

Attending to the assembly: housewarming and hospitality

One of your chief responsibilities as a sacristan is to make sure that the church is accessible and comfortable for all who enter. Care should be taken so that all who cross the threshold for liturgy enter into an environment that is safe, warm and properly lighted. Signs and symbols of God's hospitality should be evident throughout. While it is the work of those parishioners charged with the care of the art and environment of the church to provide an environment that is inviting and in accord with the seasons of the liturgical year, it is you who make the house come alive for liturgy.

Before any liturgy to which you are assigned as the sacristan, arrive early and make sure that all the doors of the church building are unlocked. In addition, unlock all the various cupboards, closets and rooms that contain the books, linens, vessels, microphones and other objects that will be needed. You may also need access to certain storage areas, such as those used for music or art. All this means, of course, that you have the keys to all these locks, including keys to the rectory and the parish hall. If a security system is installed in the church, learn the code and become familiar with the workings of the system.

Once the church is unlocked, your attention focuses on basic environmental concerns. Exterior and interior lighting is turned on as needed, and the interior temperature is noted. Heating or air conditioning is adjusted, as well as the flow of fresh air through the building. On days when incense is to be used, it is a good idea to open a window or two. In areas where winter storms bring snow and ice, arrive early enough to survey all walkways and steps and take proper measures to ensure the safety of all who will be passing in and out of the church. In some parishes this may entail a call to a designated member of the parish maintenance staff. The interior floors around the entrances should also be checked to make sure that they are free of papers, boxes or other clutter.

After taking care of these basic issues of access and comfort, inspect the baptismal font and any holy water containers to be sure that they are filled with clean water. Any sheets or booklets that will be distributed should be placed at the entrances or delivered to the ushers or greeters. Any signs requesting that certain seats be kept open should be placed at this time.

Before attending to the particular needs of the liturgy at hand, the microphones should be set up where they are needed. The sound system should be turned on and the microphones checked. If portable microphones are used, check their batteries before placing them where they are available to those who will use them. Now is a good time to light any stationary candles used in the worship space, and to make sure that the candle by the tabernacle is lit.

Preparing for the liturgy at hand

Once the house of the church is attended to, you are free to get down to the business of preparing for the liturgy at hand. There are two aspects to this preparation: the first involves the objects to be used in the liturgy, and the second involves the ministers who will be present.

Give careful attention to all the objects that will be used in the liturgy. These objects will vary from time to time, but every Mass has the same basic needs. One way to think about organizing to meet these needs is to review the order of the Mass. The introductory rites, the liturgy of the word, the liturgy of the eucharist, and the communion rite each have their own particular needs. Sometimes even the concluding rite calls for special attention.

Preparations for the introductory rites
These rites may vary from season to season. Most Masses, however, begin with a procession. In preparing for the procession, pay attention to the objects that are carried in the procession and are

destined for use in the liturgy, and to the vestments worn by the ministers. Your tasks include the following:

For the servers:

- check that albs and needed cinctures are readily accessible;

- locate the processional cross;

- make sure that processional candles are clean and functional, with wicks trimmed as needed;

- locate matches;

- arrange the seating for the servers, placing hymnals or other printed materials at their seats;

- if incense is used, fill the boat with incense, place charcoal in the thurible or bowl, and light the charcoal approximately 15 minutes prior to the start of the procession; place the stand for the thurible or a pedestal for the incense bowl in the desired location.

For the ministers of the word:

- locate the book of the gospels, and mark the appropriate reading;

- locate the *Lectionary for Masses with Children*, if this is to be used in the procession;

- place hymnals in an accessible location for those ministers not carrying any objects.

For the presider:

- hang or lay out vestments appropriate for the liturgical season;

- test the microphone to be used by the presider and place it near the vestments;

- arrange presider's chair in its designated area;

- mark the sacramentary and place it in its predetermined location;

- prepare the book of the chair or other book of presidential prayers, if one is used. The presider may wish to carry this in the procession; otherwise place it at the presider's chair;

- if there is a sprinkling rite, ready the bowls and sprinklers.

Preparations for the liturgy of the word

These preparations center on the ritual books that will be used, the place of proclamation and the general intercessions:

- place the lectionary at the ambo, open to the day's readings;

- adjust the ambo microphone (which should already have been turned on and tested);

- locate copies of the general intercessions and place one copy in a predetermined place for the reader to use during the liturgy, leave one copy in the sacristy for the reader to look over before Mass, and provide one copy for the presider.

Preparations for the liturgy of the eucharist

The preparations for the liturgy of the eucharist center on the items needed at the altar, as well as on the needs of the eucharistic ministers:

• place on one large plate an amount of bread, and fill a pitcher with an amount of wine, appropriate for the estimated number of communicants;

• place the bread and wine in a location easily accessible at the time of the preparation of the altar;

• set out on a side table the corporal and the cup that will be used during the eucharistic prayer;

• set out on a side table the required number of plates, cups and purificators for use during the distribution of communion;

• set out on a side table the bowl of water used for the washing of the presider's hands, and a towel;

• position the sacramentary to be accessible to the server;

• set out on a side table a large cloth to be used later to cover the vessels after the distribution of communion;

• unlock the tabernacle or place the key in a predetermined, accessible location

Preparations for the blessing and dismissal

Make sure that the text of any announcements is in the designated place. In addition, if there is to be a special blessing, the sacramentary needs to be made available to the presider. Find out if there will be a guest speaking at the end of the Mass in order to better facilitate the dismissal.

Attending to the needs of those who serve at the liturgy

Having finished the preparations involving the objects of the liturgy, now shift your focus to the people who minister to the assembly at the liturgy. These ministers have already been prepared for their ministry; however, you should be available to be of service, guiding them if necessary in their tasks.

While waiting for the arrival of the ministers who have been scheduled for a particular liturgy, consult any notes regarding any special features of the upcoming liturgy. If the parish liturgical coordinator is available, this might be a good time for a joint review. Ideally, as the sacristan you have participated in the preparatory meetings and discussions and are aware of the order of service and seasonal needs. However, special and last-minute needs do arise—for example, an unexpected change of presider, or cancellation of the children's liturgy of the word. Perhaps it is the first Sunday of a new liturgical season and there will be a change in the introductory rites. You might remind the liturgical ministers of the change and how it might affect their ministry.

As the ministers arrive, greet each one and take some time to answer any questions. All the while, keep an eye on the clock, coordinating the preparation of the ministers so that the procession begins in a timely manner.

At this time, between the arrival of the ministers and the beginning of the procession, your actions may involve the following:

• helping the servers vest, and directing them in the lighting of the processional candles (and the incense, if needed) and the retrieving of the processional cross;

• reminding the lector to carry the book of the gospels;

• assisting the presider with vesting, if needed, and attending to any specific needs he may have;

• noting the number of ministers of communion present;

• assisting the lectors with questions about the readings;

• finding last-minute substitutes for absent ministers;

• keeping an eye on the assembly, in case additional bread or wine may be needed;

• signaling all to move into place for the procession.

When all is ready, you move with all the ministers to the place from which the procession begins.

Facilitating the beginning of the liturgy

It may be up to you to arrange the ministers in their proper order for the entrance procession, and to give those ministers who are not carrying any liturgical object a hymnal opened to the entrance song. When all are in their places, signal the cantor that the entrance song may begin. If incense is to be used, fill the thurible at this time.

The sacristan works to help the ministers create an unhurried, steady, flowing procession by timing the point at which each minister enters the procession. Any directions given at this time are best done subtly, without exaggerated or distracting gesture. A procession that is deliberately paced, with an appropriate distance between the ministers, is a sign to all who have gathered that their liturgy begins with reverence and grace, that their liturgy is cared for and prepared. When the members of the assembly know this, they are more often than not glad to arrive on time, ready to be present for the entrance song and the other introductory rites.

Once the procession has begun, you are free to join the members of the assembly for the liturgy. Ever watchful, the sacristan remains ready to offer any needed assistance. Sometimes things do go awry—the sound system may stop working, a vessel may be dropped, needed papers may be misplaced. Perhaps a member of the assembly may fall ill. In all such cases, the sacristan takes action, doing whatever is needed with a balanced sensitivity to the situation and the action of the liturgy. In some parishes, where there are multiple Sunday Masses, the sacristan may not be required to remain with the assembly for each liturgy. Rather, the sacristan may enjoy some well-deserved "down time" between the introductory and concluding rites.

Cleaning up

At the conclusion of the liturgy, you oversee the rearrangement of the church for the next liturgy. Some of your tasks at this time might include the following:

- depositing the collection in the parish safe;

- assisting the ministers of communion with the consumption of remaining consecrated bread or wine as needed;

- overseeing the cleaning of the vessels used during the Mass, and their return to their proper places;

- collecting ritual books and returning them to their proper places;

- collecting and emptying the thurible and returning it, along with the incense boat, to its proper place;

- gathering and hanging up vestments as needed, setting aside those to be laundered;

- collecting and storing microphones;

- collecting all used communion linens for laundering.

After the last liturgy of the day, you close the house of the church. In addition to the above tasks, your work includes the following:

- lock the tabernacle;

- close and lock all cabinets containing liturgical vessels;

- extinguish all candles used during the liturgy;

- return all matches or lighters, charcoal, incense and tongs to their proper storage area;

- turn off sound, heating, air conditioning and lighting systems;

- close and lock the windows and the outside doors of the church;

- engage the security system, if one is installed.

Working relationships

In order to be effective in your ministry as sacristan, you need to develop and maintain relationships with a wide array of people.

Working with the liturgy coordinator

In many parishes, the sacristan is supervised by, and reports to, the parish liturgy coordinator. In other parishes, the music director or the pastoral associate may be the sacristan's main contact with the parish leadership. When working with a liturgy coordinator, keep the following points in mind.

• The liturgy coordinator is likely to be a member of the pastoral team or staff, and his or her responsibilities will vary depending on whether the position is full-time or part-time. The liturgy coordinator may not have full responsibility for your position. The parish business manager or the pastor may also have a part to play. For example, the liturgy coordinator may not have the authority to make changes to your job description, give you a raise in salary or approve time off. Learn how your parish has distributed leadership and oversight responsibilities regarding your position.

• Communication with the liturgy coordinator is of critical importance. At the outset, make sure that your job description is clear and unambiguous. Make sure that any expectations about your schedule and attendance at meetings are spelled out. Learn the procedures for dispute resolution.

• Learn and respect the history of your parish's leadership structure. In many cases, the positions of liturgy coordinator and sacristan may be new, and it may take some time for working relationships to settle into place.

Working with the music director

The music director is an integral member of the liturgy team. For the most part, your responsibilities do not overlap with those of the music director. However, in some cases, you and the director may need to coordinate.

• You may be responsible for some aspects of preparing the sound systems, or placing of seating or equipment.

• The music director should provide you with a list of the music for the liturgy and should inform you of any changes that may impact the flow of the liturgy, especially the several processions.

• The music director should make any specific concerns and requests known to both you and the liturgy coordinator well in advance of the time of the liturgy.

Working with presiders

Many larger parishes routinely have more than one priest who presides at the various Sunday liturgies, but many other communities have only their pastor or a visiting priest as their sole presider. Whatever the situation in your parish, presiders and sacristans need to develop good, professional working relationships. An effective presider, like any other effective minister, comes prepared, prayerful and ready to serve the assembly. Part of your job is to anticipate the practical needs of the presider and thus help him to focus on his ministry of presiding at the liturgical prayer of the gathered assembly. The presider's time before the liturgy begins is best spent in centering and transition, rather than in last-minute practicalities. Avoid peppering the presider with questions, comments or small talk. Your questions regarding the day's liturgy should be directed to the liturgy coordinator. Other pressing points about the parish's liturgical life should be discussed at a scheduled appointment during the week.

Every presider has certain unique mannerisms, preferences and needs. Anticipate and prepare for these. For example, one presider may be counted on to enter the sacristy early to review the texts for the Mass. Another may have certain preferences regarding vesture. Still another may need help with the portable microphone or with adjusting the sound system for his voice.

While these practical concerns, and others like them, are of some importance, they can be distracting or frustrating to the presider if he needs to deal with them by himself. The sacristan who learns the habits of those who regularly preside at the parish liturgies and anticipates their needs performs a valued service to the presider and the assembly. The attentive sacristan facilitates the prayer of those he or she serves.

If the presider is the pastor, keep in mind the rest of his parish responsibilities. In most parishes, the pastor is quite over-worked and he may from time to time arrive at the sacristy tired or preoccupied. Often, the attitude and disposition of the pastor set the tone for the parish and its liturgy. But this is not to say that the liturgy depends on the pastor or derives from his disposition. Most pastors understand that the liturgy is a shared endeavor, and welcome the help and guidance of the sacristan. Your sustained and reliable efforts to prepare a clean, ordered, calm environment will be seen as a wonderful gift and will bear fruit in the prayer of the presider.

Working with other ministers

In the course of your work on Sunday morning, you will interact with a wide variety of other ministers. There will be ushers, lectors, altar servers, ministers of communion, musicians, choir members, catechists, preachers and deacons, adults and children, married couples, single people and members of religious communities. Your task is to help each one enter into the liturgy in a way that is grace-filled and stress-free.

Most liturgical ministers are not employees of the parish; they are volunteers who give freely of their time and talents, and who come to serve the liturgy out of faith and love. They come from a variety of households and personal situations, and many have made sacrifices in their personal lives in order to serve their brothers and sisters in prayer. Be considerate and respectful; act more as one who hopes to be of service than one in a position of authority.

Some ministers will be well-prepared and self-confident; others will need some help and reassurance. Show them what they may need to know to be confident in their ministry, and be sure to tell them when they have touched you with their ministry. Although you may need to offer some gentle correction from time to time, leave any critique of their ministry to the parish liturgy coordinator.

Set a good example for the younger ministers, especially the younger servers. It is likely that they will look to you for direction, but you are not their director! Show them by your actions what real serving is all about. Correct them gently if needed, and praise them generously when they have served well.

Working with parish members at large

By necessity, the sacristan is often the first on the scene and the last to leave. Parishioners who regularly participate in the parish's liturgies will become accustomed to your presence. As a minister, you will become associated with the liturgy of your parish. Be respectful of the gathered assembly by dressing appropriately for the liturgy. Put your best self forward.

It is important for you to model the attitudes and actions that the liturgy encourages and requires, especially those of concern and compassion for the assembled Body of Christ. The assembly is a mixed group of believers with diverse expectations and expressions of piety. Reverence in word and action is a good rule for all those who work in the parish's liturgical space.

When you ask parish members to provide a particular service—such as bringing the bread and the wine to the altar, or carrying a banner in a procession—do not put them on the spot. Ask gently, and always allow them to decline without feeling guilty. Remember to thank all those you ask.

From time to time you may be asked questions about the day's liturgy or the liturgical practices of the parish. When you are able to do so, answer questions directly and honestly, without editorial comment. Don't hesitate to suggest a telephone call to the parish office if the questioner seeks more information or explanation.

The best thing that you can do for the assembly is to make ready a place that is inviting, hospitable and prayerful. Minimize or eliminate last-minute setting-up in the worship space. Time your work so that all is ready before the arrival of the members of the assembly. Eleventh-hour busyness always runs the risk of giving the wrong impression that the liturgy is like an assembly line, theatrical performance or fast-food restaurant. A space prepared in advance with all that the community needs for its liturgy strongly and clearly communicates the importance and value of the assembly it welcomes.

THE LITURGICAL YEAR

One of the greatest challenges for those who prepare liturgies throughout the year, year after year, is to be drawn into a given liturgy or into a given season of the liturgical year. The parish liturgy team prepares for liturgies so far in advance, and needs to tend to so many variable (and often minute) elements, that it can be difficult at times for members to celebrate the liturgy at hand. Attending to future plans and details can overshadow the present celebration of the church's prayer. There is also the danger that repeated tasks and liturgies can blend into one another in the minister's mind so that the uniqueness of each celebration is lost. In addition, the intensive work that is needed to prepare the parish's liturgies may make liturgy feel like little more than a job.

One source of help with all of this is the liturgical year itself. The seasons of the church's liturgical year are marked by prayers, rituals and scripture readings with specific qualities, emphases and tones. A good way for the hardworking sacristan to remain grounded in the liturgical prayer of the community is to remain acutely aware of the seasons of the liturgical year. The sacristan's ministry gets much of its shape and content from these seasons. They are reliable posts to which the sacristan can anchor his or her liturgical life and ministry.

From another perspective, too, the liturgical year merits the professional attention of the sacristan. In cooperation with the liturgy coordinator and the parish liturgy commission, the sacristan helps to prepare how the parish will keep the liturgical seasons in its liturgies. The sacristan must know and be able to navigate with some confidence the currents of the seasons of the liturgical year. Each season has its own rites, prayers and readings. Often there are special actions and objects particular to a given season. To be most effective, the sacristan needs to learn something of the language, feeling and purpose of each season.

Advent

Advent is a time of joyful expectation and preparation for both our celebration of the incarnation of Christ and the coming of Christ at the end of time. On the first Sunday of Advent we begin a new liturgical year, and begin reading a new set of scripture readings from the three-year cycle of readings in the lectionary. We hear in the gospels of Jesus' admonition that his disciples remain alert and watchful, of John the Baptist's life and preaching, and of Jesus' conception. Advent weekdays celebrate saints and martyrs such as Andrew, Francis Xavier, Ambrose and Lucy, and one constant companion is Mary, the mother of God. The solemnity of the Immaculate Conception (December 8) always falls during Advent, as does the feast of Our Lady of Guadalupe (December

12), with some parishes having large celebrations on this day. The celebration of *Las Posadas* ("Lodgings") by members of Mexican communities or of the *Simbang Gabi* novena by Filipino parishioners fills Advent up to Christmas Eve. The introductory rites during the Masses of Advent are often expanded to include the blessing of an Advent wreath and the lighting of its candles.

Throughout Advent, make sure that appropriate seasonal vesture for the presider is clean and pressed. Keep the liturgical space free of unnecessary objects, papers and clutter. Become familiar with the choreography of the introductory rites, especially if these involve the lighting of Advent candles. A walk through the rites with the liturgy coordinator and the presiders will be invaluable. The Advent wreath and its candles should be tended to before and after each liturgy. Families or other members of the assembly may be recruited to light the candles, and they may benefit from a brief practice beforehand. Servers, too, may need instruction about any changes to their normal routines.

Christmas

Christmas Eve and Christmas Day can be very hectic times for the sacristan. If the parish is large, these days alone can make clear the need for more than one sacristan on staff. The sacristans and the liturgy coordinator need to negotiate expectations for these days thoughtfully and develop a plan that prioritizes actions and tasks.

It is important to keep Advent clear of Christmas. In no case should the environment and art for Christmas be put in place before the final liturgy of the last Sunday of Advent. Those involved with the environment and art should be in communication with the sacristan so that their work will not have to be moved or rearranged. Ideally, the environment for the Christmas Masses will be arranged before the sacristan arrives to set up for the Christmas liturgies.

In some parishes it is not unusual to have three Masses on Christmas Eve—one for preschoolers, one for families and a midnight Mass. Included in any one of these may be once-a-year parish traditions such as lessons and carols, or a nativity play. Any of these will have their own set of requirements for the sacristan. In addition, the sacristan will attend to the amount of bread and wine to be prepared, seating arrangements to accommodate larger attendance, candles, the sound system, heating and ventilation.

One of the most important things to remember about Christmas is that it is the only day that some people come to Mass during the course of a year. Because of this, all those involved with the parish liturgy must extend a particularly gracious welcome and warm hospitality. This is a day for the warmest greeters at the doors and the friendliest ushers inside. It is a day when any music handouts should be carefully prepared and distributed to all. Do everything you can to promote and encourage this welcoming spirit.

Epiphany

This feast of the Christmas season continuing the celebration of the mystery of the incarnation calls for a luminous treatment. Extra candles may be placed around the church. Be sure that all the candles are standing tall and burning bright. Candleholders should be cleaned and polished.

Lent

The season of Lent plunges us into forty days of prayer, fasting and almsgiving that lead to the liturgies of the Easter Triduum. This season is filled with images and symbols of power and beauty. On Ash Wednesday the faithful pour through the doors to receive a gritty mark of ash as a sign of their repentance. The Sundays of Lent that follow lead us up the road to Jerusalem.

Like Advent, the season of Lent brings its own demands for the sacristan. Palm Sunday is celebrated with processions, palms and often incense. This liturgy is usually very well attended; sacristans must plan accordingly. The distribution of palms before the liturgy, the organization of the route for the procession and instructions for the servers who lead the way are just some possible items on your list of things to do.

Triduum

Driven by powerful actions and texts and illuminated through dramatic symbol, the rites of the Triduum are unrivaled in their passion and joy. Preparation for these liturgies is aimed at moving the community into these days as fully and whole-heartedly as possible.

For first-time sacristans the intensity of the Triduum can be a bit of a shock. For the parish liturgy team, it can become all-consuming. Careful preparation can help ease the strain. Nevertheless, long hours will be spent carrying out the work of these days and nights. The sacristan is an invaluable part of the parish's experience of these days, and it is best to have two sacristans for each liturgy whenever possible. Preparation meetings should always include the sacristans, liturgy coordinator, music director and the presiders for each liturgy. A rehearsal involving all the scheduled liturgical ministers is absolutely essential. No amount of reading or study can substitute for physically practicing the various liturgies. It is crucial to rehearse the timing and pace of the movements, processions, readings, prayers and music.

Easter and Pentecost

People love to come to church on Easter Sunday. As on Christmas, many who are absent for the rest of the year come on this day. Greeters and ushers should be out in full force, and more bread and wine than usual will need to be prepared. The Easter candle should be lit for every liturgy during the Easter season.

The Easter season is a time for abundance in all things—candles, water, chrism, plants, flowers, hangings, vesture, incense. Your challenge is to replenish inventories throughout the fifty days to come.

A most appropriate option for the introductory rites during this season is the rite of blessing and sprinkling of water before the Gloria and opening prayer. Be sure that all the materials for this rite are prepared and accessible, whether one bucket and sprinkler is used by the presider alone, or whether several bowls of water and freshly cut and tied branches are used. You may also be assigned to choose and briefly prepare those who will carry bowls and sprinkle the members of the assembly. In addition, the servers often need to be prepared for their role in this rite.

The fire of the Easter Vigil leads to the flames of Pentecost. Many parishes use banners, windsocks, kites and the like to celebrate Pentecost, and you need to have ready whatever fabrics and other materials will be carried in the processions of this day. Pentecost is also a wonderful day for liturgical dance and you may be called upon to help facilitate this.

Ordinary Time

The time outside of Christmas and its seasons, and Easter and its seasons, is Ordinary Time. This is made up of two periods: the shorter is the four to eight weeks between the Christmas season and Ash Wednesday, and the longer is the time between Pentecost and the First Sunday of Advent. In the Northern Hemisphere, the longer stretch of Ordinary Time is almost everywhere filled with the growing warmth of late spring and summer. Flowers and green foliage are often used in church buildings during this time. As the year turns toward the fall, the seasonal plants of autumn replace those of summer. The sacristan works with the environment committee to keep everything fresh.

One of the blessings of summer and autumn Ordinary Time is the opportunity it affords to "get things right." It is the perfect time to recruit and train new sacristans, and for veterans to reconnect with the ebb and flow of the assembly's prayer. Ordinary Time is a period of repeated forms and actions, and in its many Sundays the structure and rhythm of the liturgy can be discovered and learned by heart. Ordinary Time provides a good and extended opportunity for new sacristans to learn the patterns of the ministry. By November, they will be at home with the liturgy and ready to welcome the new challenges of Advent.

The rich variety to be found in the environment for the liturgy, as well as the church's cycles of rites and prayer over the course of the liturgical year, are both challenging and comforting to the sacristan. Just as important as understanding and working with the environment and the rites is the work of maintaining in good repair the many objects used in the liturgy. In the next chapter we will take a closer look at the storehouse and pantry of the church's liturgical space—the sacristy.

THE SACRISTY

For as long as the members of Christian communities have gathered to celebrate their rites of praise and thanksgiving, they have found it useful to designate rooms near their gathering spaces for the storage of the books, vessels, candles, oil and vesture used during their liturgies. Over the centuries, the relationship of these storage rooms to the spaces used for the liturgy has changed, reflecting the understanding of the liturgy prevalent at the time. In our own day, the location, if not the character, of the sacristy generally varies according to the construction date of the parish building. In churches built before the end of the Second Vatican Council (1965), a sacristy is almost always found off one or both sides of where the altar is situated. Most such churches have two sacristies, one intended primarily for the clergy and containing such items as liturgical books, vestments, vessels and altar linens, and another—often called the "work sacristy"—for servers and other ministers, containing objects such as vases, candles, banners, kneelers, thuribles, charcoal, incense, seasonal items and the like. These churches were designed for a liturgy that had become less the participatory and active work of the whole assembly and more the act of the clergy with a merely attentive laity. The sacristan's service in such a liturgy was not primarily directed to the whole assembly but rather to the clergy, whose actions took place in the area immediately surrounding the altar. Sacristies, therefore, came to be located adjacent to the altar.

In churches currently under construction or renovation that are designed to facilitate all Christ's faithful taking that "full, conscious, and active part in liturgical celebrations which is demanded by the very nature of the liturgy" (CSL, 14) the sacristy has a different character and location. The sacristan is here understood to minister to the whole assembly, and the sacristies are consequently often located throughout the building, dependent on the various needs of the assembly. For example, to facilitate greetings and participatory entrance processions, a room for vesting and the storage of vestments and the objects used during the entrance procession might be located near the entrance to the building. Rooms for the vessels needed for the celebration of the eucharist, and for the diverse objects needed for the celebration of baptism, might be located closer to where the materials will be needed. Still other more peripheral rooms might be used to provide convenient work space and storage for fabrics, flowers, music, instruments and the like. Whatever the configuration of sacristies, in order to be effective the sacristan must use the available spaces to their maximum potential in response to the needs of the assemblies that gather to celebrate the liturgy.

The inventory of the sacristies will vary from church to church, but every sacristy contains some of the same basic items. Most sacristans inherit their sacristies; few are in the position of designing their sacristies from scratch. In either case, it is a good idea for the sacristan to be thoroughly familiar with the contents of the parish's sacristies. A basic inventory of a sacristy located near the altar typically includes the following items: vessels and textiles, bread and wine, altar linens, vestments, oils and chrism, thuribles and incense boats, charcoal, water bucket and sprinkler, processional candles and cross, a small library of ritual books, some reference books, matches or lighters. Extra candles are often kept in this room, or in a cool room nearby. Here, too, are the microphones and extra batteries. Supporting objects also may be found here: clean towels, dish soap, laundry bag, memo pads, pens and pencils, paper clips and markers. A working fire extinguisher should always be easily accessible.

Objects that are used during the celebration of baptism, such as clean towels, candles, water pitchers, oil and chrism, may be stored in this sacristy or near the font. Cleaning supplies for candles and candle holders, wax remover, broom, dustpan and upright or hand-held vacuums all need a place of their own.

Supplies for the care and arrangement of plants and flowers also need storage space. A basic tool set, miscellaneous hardware, scissors, tape, floral arranging supplies, an assortment of vases and baskets, an iron and ironing board and a bag of clean sand are all useful. Seasonal banners or fabrics should be stored in another room whenever possible.

Maintaining order and keeping the sacristy and other workrooms neat and clean is an important part of the sacristan's ministry. A sufficient inventory of wine, incense, charcoal and candles should be maintained at all times.

Ritual and reference books

The sacristy contains within it a small library of the ritual books used at Mass: the lectionary, the book of the gospels and the sacramentary. Most sacristies also have copies of the *Lectionary for Masses with Children*.

Here, too, are the books used during the celebration of other liturgies. These most often include the following: *Rite of Baptism for Children*, *Rite of Marriage*, *Rite of Christian Initiation of Adults* and *Order of Christian Funerals*. A copy of the *Rite of Penance* and of *Pastoral Care of the Sick* are also often available.

In addition to these heavily-used ritual books, this library contains books that are consulted infrequently or only for reference purposes. These might include the *Book of Blessings* or *Catholic Household Blessings and Prayers*, hymnals, a local ordo, pamphlets of general intercessions, and other sourcebooks of prayer texts and seasonal writings. Of course, any or all of these materials will be available in each of the languages used in a given parish.

Every book that is used during the liturgy should be worthy of its role: It should be hardbound, clean, well-finished and intact. Lectionaries and books of the gospels should be the large ritual editions, not the smaller study editions. Looseleaf sheets of any kind should not be used during the liturgy.

Vessels for communion

A closet or a cupboard is usually set aside in the sacristy to store all the vessels used at Mass. These would include large plates for the bread and pitchers for the wine, smaller plates and cups for communion, small bottles for water and a bowl to be used when the presider washes his hands.

The sacristan is often in a position to put together a collection of communion vessels, and there are many appropriate choices to be found in the retail marketplace. With a little investigation and patience, matched sets of plates and cups can be found that will serve the parish well. Care should be taken to select vessels that support *ritual* dining, which means that the plates and cups should be larger and heavier than those ordinarily used at a family dining room table. Parishes sometimes purchase items more suitable for formal dinners than for public banquets. Delicate stemware, while perhaps exquisite and refined, is too small and fragile for the cup expected to hold an ample amount of the consecrated wine and meant to be passed from hand to hand.

Look for vessels that reflect the hand of their maker, without excessive decoration or imagery that narrows or directs the experience of their use. Likewise, work to build up sets of vessels of various styles and made of a variety of materials, including metal, ceramic and glass. Sacristans are also in a position to guide the parish away from using vessels that suggest that any individual or group has a personal, proprietary interest in the eucharist. Those vessels are best that through their common size and material communicate that the eucharistic liturgy is the prayer of the whole assembly.

Care in cleansing the vessels is an important responsibility of the sacristan. A procedure for this should be developed and implemented under the guidance of the sacristan. For the storage of the vessels, the parish should invest in specially made felted or quilted china protectors; these will help protect its communion ware for years to come.

Bread and wine

While some parishes have members who bake bread fresh for every liturgy, most still order wafers in quantity from specialty providers. These wafers need to be kept in a secure, dry place.

One usual task of the sacristan, whether wafers or locally baked fresh bread is used, is to set out the amount needed for a particular Mass. This is a significant task because it is most important that the members of the assembly receive the Body of Christ in bread consecrated *at the same Mass they celebrate*. In parishes that use fresh bread, by necessity this is the norm. The loaves are formed with a predetermined and uniform number of lightly scored pieces, and the recipe the bakers use yieds a certain amount of finished bread. This amount has been calculated according to the number of people who receive communion, determined by regular observation (see below for more on this). Thus, with freshly baked bread it is easy to set out the required amount for each Mass.

In too many parishes that use wafers, however, receiving communion from bread consecrated at the same Mass is still not the norm. Wafers consecrated at earlier Masses are routinely brought from the tabernacle during the communion rite at later Masses. This unfortunate and aberrant practice continues simply because of a lack of planning. With a little forethought, common sense and knowledge of the parish's communion patterns, this problem can be resolved. When the sacristan accepts the responsibility to become the guiding force in changing this practice, success is easily attained.

The sacristan first works to move the parish away from this practice by seeking a commitment from the parish leadership to use bread for communion that is consecrated at that same Mass. The sacristan then needs to share this commitment and its rationale with all the parish's ministers of communion.

Once this commitment is in place, the sacristan coordinates the count of those who receive communion at each of the parish Masses. This count should take place at each Mass each Sunday for a couple of months, and should include all those that receive communion, both adults and children. Ushers or other parish members stationed throughout the church count those receiving communion and report their results. Over the course of the weeks, an average number for each Mass will be ascertained that can be used as the basis for the number of wafers to be put out for that Mass. This same number is used to guide the bakers in those parishes where bread is baked fresh for each Mass.

When communion wafers arrive from the supplier they are often packed in bags containing several hundred wafers. Many suppliers ship bags of 500 wafers. The sacristan needs to recount these wafers into smaller, more manageable bags, perhaps containing 50, 75 or 100 wafers, depending on the size of the assembly being served. The smaller bags are then labeled, sealed and stored. When it is time for the sacristan to put out the wafers for Mass, the smaller bags make it easier to put out the correct number of wafers.

If the sacristan has carefully maintained the flow of wafers or freshly baked bread into the Mass, the consumption of any remaining wafers or pieces of bread after the Mass will not be a great problem. The sacristan should check throughout the year on how much remains after communion, and should make adjustments as necessary. Good communication with the ministers of communion and a watchful eye are very important. A written log of the amount of wafers or bread initially set out and the amount actually needed (particularly on holidays and special feasts) is an invaluable asset for the sacristan.

The sacristan also prepares the wine needed for the communion of the assembly. Wine for the Mass should be stored in a cool room. As with the bread, it is important that the sacristan know how much wine to put out for each Mass. Every effort should be made to encourage all to drink of the cup of blessing. At no time should it seem that we are skimping when it comes to the cup.

In far too many parishes an inadequate amount of wine is used. Perhaps such small amounts of wine are provided in an effort to avoid having the ministers consume a large quantity after Mass. However, providing too little wine actually discourages people from receiving from the cup. If a cup is only a quarter or third filled, not even the first people to receive communion will take much more than a drop. And few of those following will likely do anything more. Having only a little wine available works to discourage communion from the cup and in many cases leaves more for the ministers to consume. It may seem counter-intuitive, but when it comes to communion from the cup, having more wine available in the beginning often means having less remaining after

Mass because the abundance encourages people not only to approach the cup in the first place, but to draw from it an amount of some substance. A cup of abundance invites ample participation.

Altar cloths

The sacristy should contain a sufficient supply of good quality altar cloths. Ideally, the altar cloths will be custom-fitted to cover the surface of the altar. Linen and fine woven cotton are the materials of choice. The altar cloths should be elegant, and any embellishment, pattern or color scheme should be subtle and never overpowering. Poorly fitting altar cloths that hang over the edges or fall to the floor should be avoided.

Linens and other cloths used during Mass

Several different cloths are used during Mass. These include the corporal (the cloth spread immediately under the eucharistic vessels on the altar), purificators (napkin-sized cloths used to wipe the lip of the cup after each communicant drinks) and hand towels. In addition, a larger cloth is needed to cover the vessels after communion as they await their cleaning. All of the cloths used at Mass need to be clean and pressed, preferably unstarched, and made of materials that will launder well and stand up to repeated use over time. Linen, the traditional material used for these items, is the best choice. However, it is possible to find other suitable materials, such as cotton or cotton blended with linen. Always avoid cloths made of nylon or polyester as they are not absorbent.

The sacristan sets out an adequate supply of purificators before Mass, at least one per cup per Mass, with extras available if needed. A corporal and hand towel will also be needed. After Mass, the sacristan makes sure that all the used linens and other cloths are gathered together and placed in a designated area for laundry pick-up.

Miscellaneous linens and towels

In addition to preparing and caring for the cloths used during Mass (corporals, purificators, hand towels), the sacristan is also responsible for various other linens and cloths. Every sacristy should have an ample supply of hand towels kept somewhere near the sink. A supply of larger white towels suitable for use during baptism should be kept along with the other baptism supplies. A separate cache of thick white towels for use during the foot-washing of Holy Thursday is also a necessity.

Vestments

The sacristy wardrobe contains the vestments worn by the ministers during the liturgy. The vestments used at Mass are the alb, the stole, the dalmatic and the chasuble. The alb is an ankle-length white robe, and is the basic vestment of Catholic liturgy; it may be worn with a cincture (a rope-like belt) if necessary. In many parishes the alb with cincture is the regular vesture of the Mass servers. The stole is a long, scarf-like vestment worn by ordained ministers. Deacons wear the stole over the left shoulder, drawn across the chest and back, and joined on the lower right side. Other ordained ministers wear it around the neck, hanging down in front. The dalmatic is the outer vestment of the deacon, worn over the alb and stole, and the chasuble is the outer vestment proper to the priest at Mass. The style and design of the chasuble determines whether the stole is worn under it or is placed over it. Dalmatics and chasubles come in all the liturgical colors.

The watchful sacristan ensures that all the liturgical vestments reflect the spirit and timbre of the liturgical season. Mass-produced vestments are available on the commercial market in a wide range of styles, colors and materials, and their prices can range from economical to exorbitant. However, beautiful handmade vestments can often be commissioned for the price of mass-produced offerings. When choosing vestments for the parish, buy the finest

ones that the parish can afford. Understated elegance is the rule. Color and pattern should be simple. Likewise, avoid purchasing matching sets that coordinate vestments with banners and altar cloths. These draw unnecessary and typically unflattering focus to selected objects, or call attention to themselves and distract from the actions of the presider and the assembly.

All albs, dalmatics and chasubles should be hung on sturdy hangers. Stoles may likewise be hung, or folded once at the neck seam and laid flat in oversized drawers. The size of each alb should be clearly marked. A separate closet for the albs and cinctures used by the servers is advisable. One of the hallmarks of an attentive sacristan is that all the parish's vestments are clean and pressed.

Other articles of liturgical vesture include the cope, the humeral veil, and the funeral pall. The cope is a great cloak or cape, completely open in the front with a clasp at the neck. It is worn over the alb. The cope may be used by deacons or priests when presiding at liturgies other than Mass (for example, at the baptism of children, marriage, Morning or Evening Prayer, eucharistic exposition). Lay ministers serving as cantors, and as presiders at Morning or Evening Prayer or at orders of blessing, may also wear a cope. The humeral veil is a shawl-like vestment with a chain clasp in the front at the neck. It is used to cover the hands when certain vessels or objects are carried. For example, it is worn by the deacon or priest when holding the monstrance or ciborium for the blessing during eucharistic exposition, and when carrying the vessels containing the reserved eucharist on Holy Thursday and Good Friday. The funeral pall is a piece of white fabric used to cover the coffin as part of the reception of the body at the funeral vigil or Mass. The parish should have several palls in sizes for use with coffins for children and adults.

Candles

There are few objects that call up memories of the house of the church as powerfully as candles. Present at every Mass, shining at the great Easter Vigil, humbly flickering in devotion spaces—candles of various dimensions are a main staple of every church building.

Every sacristan learns quickly that keeping watch over the supply, use and maintenance of candles is an important part of the job. Inventory is especially important here, as candles are always in demand. Sacristans need to learn which candles are used when and where. Seasonal changes, as well as the needs presented by occasional prayer services or liturgies, should be noted. The following is a partial list of the various candles needed by a parish:

• paschal candle: the largest candle in the church; it is lit at the great Easter Vigil and kept burning throughout the Easter season, as well as at every baptism and funeral;

• candles for Mass: of various sizes; used regularly in procession and near the altar;

• votive candles: small candles used in devotional areas;

• candles for the members of the assembly: generally short or thin and tapered candles held by those in the assembly, especially during the Easter Vigil, Evening Prayer and other occasional prayer services; used with an accompanying collar or shield to catch dripping wax;

- baptism candles: of various sizes; distributed at every baptism;

- special candles: of various sizes and colors; held or used in table or floor candelabra or special holders during feasts and holidays (for example, in Advent wreaths, on the feast of the Presentation, for the blessing of throats on the feast of Saint Blase).

In addition, every sacristy should have a supply of candle-lighting tapers—wick-sized waxed strings either held by hand or inserted in a holder or candle-lighting pole, used to light other candles.

It is important that all candles be stored in a cool, dry and clean location. Keep the candle storage room in good order, and try to keep candles sorted according to purpose and size. Candle suppliers often buy back the stub remains of burnt candles, so it is wise to have a container for this type of recycling.

Art and environment supplies

Few churches are fortunate enough to have a separate workroom and storage area for their art and environment needs and supplies. In most parishes, the sacristy and any available space in any adjoining room is used for this purpose. One essential item for the sacristy is a well-stocked toolbox; basic tools, scissors and tapes are minimum requirements. Items used for floral arranging should also be on hand: stem cutters, floral foam, wire, tape, baskets, vases and other containers.

Banners and their accompanying hardware such as standards and cross bars also need a place. The banners should be organized and stored according to the seasons in which they are used. Some churches have special closets designed for the hanging storage of banners. Otherwise, rolling banners on cardboard tubes is a good way to minimize creasing. Be sure to protect all hangings from dirt and dust by wrapping them loosely in plastic during storage.

Don't allow the art and environment materials to take over the sacristy. Find a separate room for dried flowers, vases and other containers, Advent wreaths, nativity scenes and other items used only once a year. The sacristy is not just a storeroom. It is the staging area for every parish liturgy, and it must be kept clean and clear of clutter if it is to be most effectively used for this purpose.

THE TRIDUUM

The liturgical year both culminates in and flows from the days of the paschal Triduum—from the evening Mass of the Lord's Supper on Holy Thursday to Evening Prayer on Easter Sunday. The liturgies of the Triduum—so rich with scripture, prayer, procession, symbol, music, action and gesture—challenge the parish to allow all the time and energy necessary for their fullest expression. The leadership of the parish needs to work to invite the members of the assembly to dwell in the hours and days of the great Easter Triduum. The environment of these liturgies invites and expects participation, and the demands on the sacristan are great. If ever there is one, this is the time for two sacristans to be present for each liturgy if at all possible.

For unprepared sacristans, the days of the Triduum can become a nightmare of frustrating logistics. To get ready for the work of the Triduum, set aside time during Lent to read about and study the rites of Holy Thursday, Good Friday, Holy Saturday and Easter Sunday. Before Holy Week, each of the liturgies of the Triduum must be reviewed thoroughly with the parish liturgy coordinator. Rehearsals for each liturgy, with all the ministers who will be involved, are invaluable and indispensable tools.

At the conclusion of each day's liturgy, make some notes about what went well and what needs improvement. Recommendations and critiques should be shared with the parish liturgy coordinator once the Triduum is past. It takes years to get the rhythms of these days into the bones. Rejoice in the successes, and resolve to smooth out the rough spots in the coming years.

The environment for the Triduum

The sacristan can assist in the work of the parish's environment and art coordinators by preparing a clean canvas on which the Triduum may be painted. The closing weeks of Lent are perfect for a thorough spring cleaning. Start by making sure that the sacristy and the rest of the church building are clean and uncluttered. Vestments, linens and other needed cloths should be inventoried, cleaned and stored. All furniture and other objects (such as candleholders and vessels, for example) should be cleaned and polished. Keep an eye out for ways to make the church as inviting as possible. Perhaps an outdoor clean-up is in order to sweep away winter's debris. Tend to newly growing flower beds and lawns. Polish the door hardware, sweep entranceways, and be sure that all outdoor lighting is in working order for the Triduum's evening liturgies. While not all of this is the responsibility of the sacristan, it is fair to say that the sacristan's job over the Triduum will be easier if this advance work is done. A team effort by several members of the parish is the best way to accomplish these many tasks.

In addition to general preparations for the Triduum as a whole, each of the liturgies has its own special requirements.

The Holy Thursday evening Mass of the Lord's Supper

The first of the Triduum's liturgies, the evening Mass of the Lord's Supper on Holy Thursday, places a special emphasis on Jesus' command that his disciples follow his example of being servant to others: As Jesus washed the feet of the disciples, those who follow him are to go and do likewise. The meaning of this footwashing lies at the heart of what the church struggles to become, and our ritual of the washing of feet during the liturgy of Holy Thursday evening illuminates this.

Although the washing of feet is a crucial element of the liturgy of Holy Thursday evening, it is not the only unique feature. Members of the parish may process into the church with the year's newly consecrated oils, prayed over and distributed at the Chrism Mass of the diocese earlier that day or week. In addition, on this night the tabernacle in the church is emptied and the eucharistic bread is transferred to another location.

The environment for Holy Thursday

In the weeks and days before the liturgy, you will need to locate and clean the pitchers, bowls and towels that will be used during the footwashing this night. Take an inventory of what the parish has, and make a shopping list of additional items that are needed.

Like the vessels used for communion, the pitchers and bowls used for the washing of feet need to be of sizes and proportions that meet the needs of the rite. Look for simple, cleanly designed wares, pitchers and bowls capable of holding an adequate amount of water, and bowls large enough for the immersion of two feet at a time. Bowls with rims are easiest to handle. Buy as many pieces as your budget will allow, in order to compensate for any breakage. Have sufficient soap at each station.

Stock up on towels for the footwashing. A little forethought goes a long way: Watch for medium-sized white cotton towels on sale throughout the year. Since such towels have a way of disappearing from the sacristy, keep a special cache for the Triduum in storage throughout the year.

All the newly consecrated oils should be transferred to the ambry. Use vessels designed to be functional yet beautiful to the eye and touch. Remember size, proportion and the needs of the rite: Cruets intended for domestic use as containers for vinegar and salad oil, or palm-sized perfume bottles, are not adequate to the task. Vesture for this night is white.

Preparations for Holy Thursday

A good way to begin the task of preparing for the liturgy of Holy Thursday is to consider liturgy in sections, and then assign tasks to each section. Your worksheet for this night might include the following seven sections:

1. General preparations
2. Entrance procession
3. Presentation of the oils
4. Liturgy of the word
5. Washing of feet
6. Liturgy of the eucharist
7. Transfer of the eucharist

General preparations Many of the usual tasks that are performed before any liturgy likewise need to be attended to this evening. The church building is opened, lighting adjusted, sound systems checked and the necessary books are readied. Vesture, vessels, bread and wine are set out. Ministers are checked in, and hymnals or song sheets are given to the greeters and ushers for distribution.

There are additional items to prepare for this liturgy:

- vessels for the holy oils, and the place for their reservation
- soap, pitchers, bowls and towels for the washing of feet
- matches, charcoal, incense, thuribles and incense boats
- accessible procession routes
- humeral veil and vessels for the transfer of the eucharist

The entrance procession While responsibility for decisions about the formation and route of the entrance procession lies with the parish liturgy coordinator, you are responsible for all of the objects used during the procession. These include the processional cross, candles, thurible and gospel book as usual. The recently consecrated oils may also be carried in the procession and presented in the assembly. Several parish members may carry in the pitchers and bowls to be used during the washing of feet. In addition, the cantors and members of the choir may be included. Your task is to ensure that all these people have what they need, and know what to do with the objects they have as the liturgy continues. You also assist with positioning the ministers in the procession and starting the procession on time.

Presentation of the oils You may need to prepare the newly consecrated oils from the diocesan Chrism Mass. Empty and thoroughly clean the permanent vessels before transferring the new oils into them. The ambry should be spotless.

Liturgy of the word The liturgy of the word for this night takes the usual Sunday form of a first reading, responsorial psalm, second reading and gospel proclamation. Review chapter two for general preparations.

Washing of feet Your role during the washing of feet could take several forms. First is the preparation of all the needed objects— soap, pitchers, bowls and towels. Large folding tables covered with clean white tablecloths work fine as staging areas. You may also help set up chairs at the various washing stations. During the rite,

you may help refill pitchers, empty bowls and provide clean towels as needed, and you may remove the chairs as the action comes to an end.

Liturgy of the eucharist The liturgy of the eucharist follows the standard form on this night. Some parishes that do not regularly use freshly baked bread choose to do so for this Mass (and again at the Easter Vigil). If this is planned at your parish, you oversee the preparation of the bread once it arrives in the sacristy.

Transfer of the eucharist Check that each item to be used during the transfer of the eucharist — humeral veil, vessel for the eucharistic bread, thurible, incense — is in its assigned, accessible place. Incense is used in the procession out of the church and into the place of reposition. Extra charcoal will likely be required, and the sacristan should have materials (such as tongs and matches or a lighter) to light fresh charcoal as needed. In addition, prepare a candle near the tabernacle of reposition, and be sure that all doors to the place of reposition are unlocked and accessible.

At the conclusion of the liturgy, make sure that all of the objects used this night are cleaned as needed and returned to their proper places. Return all the vessels used during the footwashing to storage, and move all the towels and linens to the laundry. Tables, chairs and other stands should be removed, and the whole space—including the sacristy—made neat and clean, ready for the liturgies of Good Friday.

From the sacristan's point of view, the evening Mass of the Lord's Supper will cause few problems if it is approached with forethought and preparation. The powerful expression of service celebrated in this liturgy may well become a source of renewed energy and vision for the sacristan, whose ministry truly involves service to the prayer of the church.

The Good Friday celebration of the Lord's passion

On this night, the well-known story is told, communal prayer is offered, and the cross is venerated. A simple sharing of communion leads into the final hours preceding the great feast of Easter. Good Friday resonates deeply in the collective soul of believers. The powerful, passionate and elegant liturgy of Good Friday is less complicated for the sacristan than the other liturgies of the Triduum; nevertheless, it requires careful preparation.

The environment for Good Friday

The rites of this liturgy demand an environment that has been stripped bare. On this night it is the unadorned gestures, words, prayers and procession that beget entry and immersion into these holy hours. All of Holy Thursday's materials must be removed and put away; there is no altar cloth, no candles, no cross on or near the altar.

The centerpiece of tonight's liturgy is the veneration of the cross. Some parishes use their processional cross; others have another, larger cross made from wood, which invites a touch or a kiss. This cross may be veiled or left bare. If the option for veiling is chosen, restraint is important. This is not a night to decorate the cross. Vesture for this night is red.

Preparations for Good Friday

You may want to consider the liturgy in the following sections to aid in your preparations:

1. Liturgy of the word
2. General intercessions
3. Veneration of the cross
4. Communion

The liturgy begins simply with silent and spoken prayer. There is no entrance procession; there are no introductory rites. The community's prayer from the night before simply continues. This means that nothing is to be carried in procession, but everything needed should be made accessible at the proper time.

Liturgy of the word Make sure that the lectionary is accessible to those who will be proclaiming the readings. In some parishes the account of the passion is proclaimed with multiple readers. Whether this form is used or the passion is read by one person, it is your responsibility to see that the prepared texts are in place for the lectors, to check all microphones and to adjust the sound system.

The intercessions The texts of the special intercessions of this liturgy should be distributed to the one who will introduce each intention, to the presider who will chant or say the prayer and to the director of music. Make sure that the copies given to each person are identical.

Veneration of the cross During planning for tonight's liturgy, the procession route for the cross was determined. Make sure that this route is not impeded. Cross, candles and incense are to be prepared and made accessible for those who will carry them in procession. Light the charcoal as the intercessions begin, and place stands to receive the thuribles and candles when the veneration comes to an end. During the veneration, you may wish to sit or stand discreetly close to the cross in case a parishioner needs assistance.

Communion   There is no liturgy of the eucharist today; instead, there is communion using the bread consecrated the night before and reserved in the tabernacle of repose. Have ready an altar cloth, a corporal and candles that will be placed on or near the altar. After communion, the liturgy ends with the presider exiting quietly after the prayer over the people. At the conclusion of the liturgy, return all of the objects used to their proper places and make sure that the sacristy and church are neat and clean for the liturgies of Holy Saturday.

The great Vigil of Easter

On the night of the great Vigil of Easter, around a crackling fire, the church gathers to await the Risen One. No other liturgy so powerfully dovetails ancient traditions and rites with contemporary longings for communion and redemption. No other liturgy sets out so consciously and deliberately to draw us into the symbols of fire, water, oil, food and drink. No other night beckons, illumines, catches and converts us weary pilgrims with as much force. And on no other night is pure joy served up in such abundance.

There is really only one way for the sacristan to approach the Easter Vigil: Work toward and through this night with reverent dedication. Pledge to do the best you can, do just that, and let the rest go. Realize that this is a night full of the messiness of our humanity—of building fires and preparing baptismal baths, of telling stories in the dark and proclaiming the Good News in the light of Christ, of enjoying abundance in all things. Count on tonight to be overwhelming. It is! It's supposed to be!

The environment for the Easter Vigil

Flowers are traditional at Easter, and they serve to underscore the beauty and joy of God's promise of redemptive love. But it is important that the environment not overwhelm the actions. The art and environment are to support the ritual actions. The sacristan and parish art and environment team must understand the nature of the liturgy as an activity of the Body of Christ and work with that in mind. In this way, the art and the environment will serve the assembly's actions, supporting where and when needed, never obscuring, and never interposing distance or barriers to full participation.

The Easter Vigil calls for some special items. To begin with, special attention is to be paid to the fire and the paschal candle. The vessel holding the sacred chrism also needs attention: It should be beautiful and large enough for all to see. Candelabra may be positioned to provide light at the ambo and cantor's stand during the liturgy of the word. Processional banners, used during the gospel procession and the procession of the catechumens and assembly to the font, are a wonderful addition. Flowers and other arrangements of plants may adorn the worship space.

The much loved Easter lily has become inextricably linked to the whole Easter season, which can be a challenge to those who design and execute floral arrangements. The lily has its place, but it can be surrounded and complemented by other species of flowering plants. Consider including budding branches of apple and cherry blossoms, pussy willow and forsythia. All of these and more like them can be added to the palette. Take time to design fitting arrangements for the whole church. Simply placing a crowd of potted plants in their plastic nursery pots around the ambo, font and altar is the easy way out and unworthy of the liturgy.

Preparations for the Easter Vigil

Many special features surround the liturgies of the word and eucharist on this night. Begin preparations by reviewing the order of the liturgy with the parish liturgy coordinator and by taking part in a walk-though rehearsal of the entire liturgy. Make comprehensive notes to organize your tasks. One way to organize your thoughts is by listing what happens during this night and where it happens. One such list might look like this:

1. First things—sacristy

2. Blessing of the fire and lighting of the candle—outdoors

3. Easter proclamation (Exsultet)—indoors

4. Liturgy of the word—ambo

5. Sacraments of initiation and rite of reception into the full communion of the Catholic church—font

6. Liturgy of the eucharist—altar

First things Begin the evening by doing all that is usually required: unlock and open all the doors, and adjust the interior heating and cooling controls. The lighting scheme for the liturgy should have been worked out well in advance, and now you turn on lights according to the plan. Check the font; it should be clean and ready for baptism. Make sure the font contains hot water now. It will cool to a comfortable temperature during the liturgy of the word. Any flow of water in the font should be turned off. Take a few moments to review your working notes. If two or more sacristans are working as a team, make sure that each person has designated assignments.

Lay out the vestments to be worn by the presider. The color of the vesture is white. Extra vestments (for example, a spare alb) may be required if the presider enters the font for baptism. Ready the microphones and sound system. Make sure that the presider's book of prayers is at hand. Servers may need your assistance with their vesture, but they, like everyone else, should be practiced and ready by this time. Everything you will need this night should be placed exactly where you want it: charcoal, incense, candles, matches, tapers, thuribles and stands, vessels, books, towels, oils, bread and wine. If you have maintained order in the sacristy during the course of the Triduum, you will be ready for action.

Blessing of the fire and lighting of the candle Tonight, the liturgy begins at the fire. The Easter fire is perhaps the most distinctive and memorable element of this night. From this fire the large paschal candle is lit. From here begins the first procession of the night: a journey through the night into a darkened church. Well before the liturgy begins, the fire is prepared. A "fire keeper" is assigned to build and light the fire, as well as keep watch over it. The fire should be large enough to generate light and warmth sufficient to invite parishioners to gather around. It should be made with a hard wood that will burn throughout the night. Adding a fragrant wood, such as piñon, beckons arriving parishioners as they leave their cars or walk the church grounds. Avoid anything that suggests cooking; this night is not about barbecue! A platform for the fire may be built of bricks, or stones may form a ring around the fire. Make sure that the fire is going before the liturgy is scheduled to start.

Greeters with song sheets and congregational candles should stand ready to welcome all. Make sure that they have all that they need. Congregational candles should be counted, fitted with their accompanying collars or shields, and placed in baskets with the song sheets ahead of time, waiting for the greeters to pick them up. The sacristan will also place tongs, a taper, charcoal, thuribles and incense near the fire, along with the presider's book of prayers. It is very nice to keep the fire burning throughout the liturgy. Put one last piece of wood on during communion. As the members of the assembly flow out of the church and into the night, many will gravitate to the still-burning fire and linger there a while.

Tonight, the light of Christ is symbolized in the towering paschal candle. Thanks to this light, layers of meaning are illumined and reflected, and the light of the divine presence is made manifest in our assembly. So, yes, the paschal candle must be big! As big as your space and your budget allow. And, yes, it must be real! No wax-covered shell with a spring-loaded taper center will do. The paschal candle must be beautiful, carried with strength and dignity, and set in a stand worthy of itself. Once inside the church, the paschal candle should be placed near the font or the ambo. The sacristan must ensure that the candle is cared for properly before the liturgy, and once set in its stand it becomes one of the sacristan's most important charges. Make sure that it is topped by a good follower that fits properly, and that it always stands erect.

Easter proclamation (Exsultet) Prepare for the entrance procession into the church by adjusting the lighting to indicate clearly all the emergency exits. Except for this emergency lighting, the interior of the church should be in darkness. Small votive candles or hurricane lamps may stand near stairs and platforms to provide enough light for safe passage. Stands for thuribles and processional candles should be readied.

Liturgy of the word Tonight's liturgy calls for an extended liturgy of the word. One by one, readers proclaim ancient stories of faith, tracing the journey from creation to resurrection and to baptism into Christ Jesus. The lectionary should be ready at the ambo. Candelabra may be used there and at the cantor's stand to provide light. A hurricane lamp may be placed at the base of the ambo to light the floor if needed. The book of the gospels (with tonight's reading clearly marked) should be placed on the altar for the presider to take up at the gospel procession. Extra charcoal for the servers to add to the thurible for the gospel procession, as well as extra processional candles if desired, should be ready at a side table.

Sacraments of initiation and the rite of reception The font should have already been cleaned and filled with hot water that will have cooled to a comfortable temperature by the time of the baptisms. Near the font, place any pitchers that will be used for the pouring of water, towels and the chrism. On a side table there should be a basin of water, soap and hand towels for the presider. (Some presiders will want slices of lemon to help remove the chrism from their hands.) The newly baptized will need a place to dry off and change into their white robes. Be sure to provide plenty of towels, a hair dryer or two, robes and baptism candles. If the members of the assembly are unable to approach the font and take some of the water during their renewal of baptismal promises, the sacristan should arrange bowls and sprinklers on a side table for the presider and other ministers to sprinkle the people with the blessed water.

Liturgy of the eucharist The altar should be prepared for this evening with special attention to the altar cloth and other linens. A side table should contain all the necessary vessels, along with additional charcoal and matches if incense is to be used during the preparation of the bread and wine.

At the conclusion of the Vigil, the sacristan should attend to all the housekeeping tasks required to prepare the sacristy and the church for the liturgies of Easter Sunday. For the most part, Easter Sunday Masses follow the usual form, with the addition of the renewal of baptismal promises and the sprinkling with the blessed water. Easter Sunday in most parishes is a day of heavy attendance; greater amounts of bread and wine should be set out. The sacristan's contribution in helping create an environment that is inviting, gracious, generous and prayerful cannot be overemphasized.

Conclusion

The ministry of the sacristan is a crucial one in the life of a parish, and its importance cannot be overstated. An industrious and spirit-filled sacristan is a gift to all who cross the threshold of the church. By preparing and overseeing the things of the liturgy, readying them and rendering them accessible to the members of the assembly, the sacristan works to make the full, conscious and active participation of all at the liturgy a lived reality.

As a team player who brings the ability to follow through on the myriad of details that support liturgical action and prayer, the sacristan necessarily interacts with both liturgical ministers and liturgical things. The well-prepared and informed sacristan who competently works through the tasks of seasons and Sundays becomes an invaluable asset to the rest of the parish's ministers. The sacristan who keeps the things used during the liturgy in good working order, and who strives to make a space that welcomes the assembly, contributes to the entire parish's perception and experience of its liturgy. The hallmarks of a good sacristan—hospitality and reverence—gradually become integrated into the consciousness and practice of the entire assembly when they are modeled by a sacristan who works gracefully and diligently week after week.

Those who choose this ministry can look forward to many grace-filled opportunities to serve the gathered body of Christ, opportunities that will be as rewarding as they will be demanding. The sacristan becomes intimately bound to the liturgy, to that "summit toward which the activity of the church is directed" and the "source from which all its power flows" (*Constitution on the Sacred Liturgy*, 10). To the one who is called to this service, much is demanded, and in turn so much is given.

BIBLIOGRAPHY

Selected Resources from LTP

Sunday Mass Five Years from Now, by Gabe Huck. A step-by-step scheme for working anew toward the renewal of Sunday Mass in your parish. This book guides you to and through the church's documents and various books and videos from Liturgy Training Publications to encourage you in a sustained effort to make real in your parish the vision that the Second Vatican Council had for the church at liturgy.

The Sacristy Manual, by G. Thomas Ryan. Lists and other information that will help you set up for a variety of liturgies. Includes invaluable summaries of the documentation about how the areas of the worship space are best arranged and appointed.

Basket, Basin, Plate and Cup: Vessels in the Liturgy, edited by David Philippart. An informative collection of essays about and photos of the church's vesels.

Clothed in Glory: Vesting the Church, edited by David Philippart. A collection of photos and essays on the church's textiles: vesture for people, for the altar, even for the building. A comprehensive guide to the caring of the textiles we use in our liturgies.

To Crown the Year: Decorating the Church through the Seasons, by Peter Mazar. Here is solid, practical advice on how to adorn the church's house for the seasons of the year and during Ordinary Time, too! For the liturgy committee, the sacristan and all who work with the environment of the assembly.

Liturgy with Style and Grace, by Gabe Huck and Gerald T. Chinchar. A no-frills book about the church's worship. This book teaches us about those things that belong to all of us: the Mass, the sacraments, the seasons of the church's year. Here is a way to continue the mandate of the Second Vatican Council toward full, conscious and active participation by all the faithful.

The Communion Rite at Sunday Mass, by Gabe Huck. This book explores every aspect of the communion rite and shows how strong it can be at every Mass in every parish.

The Eucharistic Prayer at Sunday Mass, by Richard McCarron. This book examines the eucharistic prayer in a search for practical ways to re-establish its rightful place of prominence as the prayer of the assembly.